# What's Mine & What's Yours

## Jessica Butcher

T0021758

*methuen* | drama

LONDON • NEW YORK • OXFORD • NEW DELHI • SYDNEY

METHUEN DRAMA
Bloomsbury Publishing Plc
50 Bedford Square, London, WC1B 3DP, UK
1385 Broadway, New York, NY 10018, USA
29 Earlsfort Terrace, Dublin 2, Ireland

BLOOMSBURY, METHUEN DRAMA and the Methuen
Drama logo are trademarks of Bloomsbury Publishing Plc

First published in Great Britain 2022

Cover design and illustration by Rebecca Heselton

Sky photo © onajourney / Shutterstock

A catalogue record for this book is available from the British Library.

A catalog record for this book is available from the Library of Congress.

ISBN: PB: 978-1-3503-7257-3
ePDF: 978-1-3503-7259-7
eBook: 978-1-3503-7258-0

Series: Modern Plays

Typeset by Mark Heslington Ltd, Scarborough, North Yorkshire

To find out more about our authors and books visit
www.bloomsbury.com and sign up for our newsletters.

## Foreword by Emma Thompson

I first met Helen Bamber in the early 1980s when she was running her first organisation for victims of torture, and I was a part-time, mostly unpaid, stand-up comedian. I would perform at benefits for her foundation, and she would treat me for depression. We were made for each other.

From Helen and indeed from many of her clients who came from the hell of Videla's and Pinochet's torture chambers, I learnt about the nature of trauma and useful patterns of healing. Helen herself understood suffering at its deepest levels, having witnessed it in Bergen-Belsen in 1945, where she worked with the Jewish Relief Unit.

She knew how to help.

She was able to hear people's stories without evincing shock, pity or judgement. She was the only person to whom elderly, stoic Northern men could speak about the atrocities of the Japanese POW camps, because they knew she wouldn't 'mind'.

She told me that the worst thing that can happen to a person, sometimes even worse than the trauma itself, is to not be believed. This is often our way of not wanting to hear about it. If listening to the news can bring your emotions up in a nasty bruise, imagine what listening to experiences of torture can do. We prefer to avoid the anguish.

Either way, the sufferer loses their voice twice – once during the trauma, and then again in the face of others' disbelief, or fear, or even anger.

She told me that victims often felt shame about their suffering and even blamed themselves.

Many of us would like to help people who have suffered but we don't want it to be long, messy and complex. We would prefer to give sympathy or practical assistance and get it over with. But human suffering is as layered and as complex as humans.

That is what this play is about: what happens after the trauma.

Trauma of the following kinds – trafficking for domestic servitude, forced labour, sexual slavery, torture – causes the catastrophic suppression of extreme emotions. You cannot deal with them at the time. You can only endure.

When the trauma ends and the person is removed or escapes from the source, a new and vastly more insidious form of suffering begins as those emotions clamour to be heard and cannot be expressed, because of terror, shame and the doubt and fear of others.

Therefore, simply to listen to the story is the first step towards healing.

If you want to help, in an official or voluntary way, you must be able to listen, which is hard when sometimes we cannot even hear ourselves.

Helen was the best listener I have ever met.

The work of the Helen Bamber Foundation embodies all she believed in. It's sophisticated and subtle and almost impossible to sum up in the the neat sentences that the fundraising experts we worked with often wanted.

'What is it in a nutshell?' They would ask us. 'Give us something pithy, something punchy, something immediately clear.'

It was impossible to put the work into a soundbite; thus was born The Conversation, for which this play was created. The idea was to give Survivors and supporters a new way of being together.

It was designed to illuminate the work through talk and art – and at its centre was the belief that understanding the suffering of others – particularly others, as Helen would say, to whom we owe nothing – is perhaps the pinnacle of human emotional development.

It allows us to help and to heal others, and crucially it allows us to help and heal ourselves. It expands our capacity for empathy.

I believe that only by understanding how deeply, in what myriad and terrible ways we can be hurt, can we develop our instinct not to hurt others. We can also develop the capacity to listen, to be present and not to judge.

Suffering is universal and inevitable, mild or extreme, and – as Jess says – if we understand it and learn how to deal with it better, we might just change things.

*What's Mine & What's Yours* was published to coincide with its first performance at Shakespeare's Globe, The Underglobe on 29 September 2022. This performance was specifically created for The Conversation in aid of the Helen Bamber Foundation.

**Cast**

**Jessica Butcher**
**Basil Eidenbenz**
**Anoushka Lucas**
**Kerry Smith**
**Emma Thompson**
**Gaia Wise**

Written by **Jessica Butcher**

With original music written and performed by **Anoushka Lucas**

**Jessica Butcher** is a writer and an actor. Her first show, *Sparks*, which she both wrote and performed, was recorded for BBC Radio 4. *Canon*, a new musical, is co-produced by Trafalgar Entertainment. Jessica's play *September Skies* has been performed across primary schools as part of the Grenfell Well-Being for Children and Young People Fund.

Her acting credits include; *Offside* (UK tour, Edinburgh Festival), *Where Do Little Birds Go?* (Old Red Lion, UK tour, Edinburgh Festival) and *EastEnders* (BBC).

She is currently writing her first book and developing a TV show.

**Basil Eidenbenz** is a Swiss actor and an accomplished pianist.

His roles include: *Victoria* (TV), *The Witcher* (Netflix), *Indiana Jones* (film), *The Favourite* (film), *Bachman une Frisch* (film) and many more.

He is currently working on writing new material.

**Anoushka Lucas** is a singer, songwriter, actor and composer. Her music has been championed by BBC Introducing, BBC Radio 2 and Jazz FM. Her debut album *Dark Soul* was released in 2019.

As an actor, Anoushka has played Laurey in *Oklahoma!* (Young Vic), Katherine/Gower in *Henry V* (Donmar Warehouse), Katie in *After Life* (National Theatre). Her other credits include *Jesus Christ Superstar* (Regent's Park Open Air

Theatre), *Chiaroscuro* (Bush Theatre) and *Sparks* (Edinburgh Festival).

As a composer Anoushka co-created the music for *The Ballad of Klook and Vinette* (book by Ché Walker, Park Theatre/ NAMT Festival NYC), *The Etienne Sisters* (book by Ché Walker, Theatre Royal Stratford) and *Sparks* (book by Jessica Butcher, Vault Festival, Edinburgh Festival and BBC Radio 4).

**Emma Thompson** is one of the world's most critically lauded and respected talents for her versatility in acting as well as screenwriting. She is the sole artist thus far to have received an Academy Award for both acting (*Howards End*) and screenwriting (*Sense and Sensibility*).

Thompson's film credits begin with *The Tall Guy*, her feature debut in 1988. They include the aforementioned *Sense and Sensibility* (for which she also received a Best Actress Oscar nomination); *The Remains of the Day* (Oscar nomination); *In the Name of the Father* (Oscar nomination); *Last Christmas* (for which she was also co-screenwriter and producer); *Late Night*; *The Children Act*; *Love Actually*; *Saving Mr. Banks*; *The Meyerowitz Stories*; Disney's live-action *Beauty and the Beast*; *Harry Potter and the Prisoner of Azkaban*; *Harry Potter and the Order of the Phoenix*; *Henry V*; *Dead Again*; *Peter's Friends*; *Much Ado About Nothing*; *Junior*; *Carrington*; *The Winter Guest*; *Primary Colors*; *Stranger Than Fiction*; *Last Chance Harvey*; *Love Punch*; *Brave*; two of the *Men In Black* sequels; *Cruella*; *Good Luck To You, Leo Grande*; *Matilda* and *What's Love Got to Do With It*.

Thompson is President of the Helen Bamber Foundation, a UK-based human rights organisation, formed in April 2005, to help rebuild the lives of, and inspire a new self-esteem in, Survivors of gross human rights violations. On behalf of the Foundation, Thompson co-curated 'Journey,' an interactive art installation which used seven transport containers to illustrate the brutal and harrowing experiences of women sold into the sex trade. Thompson and 'Journey' travelled to

London, Vienna, Madrid, New York and the Netherlands for exhibitions and interviews.

**Gaia Wise** is an actor and writer. She primarily acts on film and television and works for charitable organisations focussed on eating disorder recovery.

Her acting credits include: *A Walk in the Woods* (film), *Last Chance Harvey* (film), *Silent Witness* (TV), *A Love Worth Fighting For* (short film), *The Lord of the Rings: The War of the Rohirrim* (film) and *Sweeney Todd* (theatre).

She is currently writing a play with Rosie Day for the Southwark Playhouse.

**A note from the author**

If you would like to learn more about how to help people, and yourself, practically manage trauma, pain and shame – have a look at The Trauma Informed Code of Conduct. You can download it for free at www.helenbamber.org/resources/best-practiseguidelines/trauma-informed-code-conduct-ticc

**Thanks from the author**

A very big thank you to Ruth Dearnley at Stop The Traffik. To Rebekah Lisgarten also at Stop The Traffik who took hours out of her incredibly busy schedule to talk to me and read an early draft.

At the Helen Bamber Foundation, I am so grateful for the time and knowledge of Rachel Witkin and Dragana Wright. Thank you also to Gareth Holmes and Alex Ciucu for trusting me with something so important.

Steven Moffett, our event producer and director, has championed this play from its very first draft. His thoughts and passion have been instrumental in it coming to life so beautifully.

And finally to Emma Thompson and Kerry Smith, thank you for having faith in me. The combined wisdom and kindness these two share leaves me wordless.

# What's Mine & What's Yours

*For the Helen Bamber Foundation*

This is a fictionalized narrative of trafficking
and not an accurate representation of a specific
Survivor's story. No real names are used.

**Part One – Body**

**Part Two – Mind**

**Part Three – Soul**

## Part One

## Body

**Anoushka**   My name is Anoushka
and I'm going to be playing the piano and the part of Mum

**Basil**   My name is Basil
and I'm going to be playing Edon, Father, Alek and the
Security Guard

**Jess**   My name is Jess
and I'm going to be playing Sally, Airport Security Woman,
Samira, the Volunteer and the Woman With The Friendly
Face and Blonde Hair

**Gaia**   My name is Gaia
and I'm going to be playing Edrina

**Emma**   And my name is Emma
and I'm going to be playing the Narrator
Okay, let's go


### Scene One – Rejecting

**Edrina**   I don't think you understand
I had no choice

**Narrator**   Edrina is sitting at a table in a small room at the
Home Office Immigration Department
she's staring at the circular water marks on the table.
Sitting on the other side of the table is a woman
her name is Sally

**Sally**   I don't think *you* understand how important this
interview is
this is the UK's Home Office and
if you really can't show me that what you're saying is true
then there's not much I can do about it.

Do you see?
We need the truth

**Edrina**    It is the truth

**Sally**    But we need *evidence* that you were trafficked here
that you came here against your will
and that if I was to send you home your life would be at risk.
I need *evidence* to understand that – otherwise there's not
much I can do.
Can you understand that?

**Edrina**    Yes I understand that
all I have is my story
and I'm telling you the truth

**Sally**    Well here's the problem Edrina,
the law in this country doesn't work with stories
it only works with facts.
And to put it simply,
your story – look it just isn't credible

**Narrator**    Edrina continues to stare at the water marks

**Edrina**    You don't believe me

**Sally** (*ignoring her and changing tactic*)    Your English isn't bad

**Edrina**    I worked hard at school

**Sally**    So you had an education in your home country?

**Edrina**    Yes

**Sally**    Why did you leave then?
You were able to get an education in your home country
why not stay?

**Edrina**    I told you I came with Alek

**Sally**    Ah yes, Alek again
so just to recap
you went from your home
in Alek's friend's car

to somewhere in Europe
you think Italy
and then you came on a plane to the UK.
Is that correct?

**Edrina**    Yes, I think so I

**Narrator**    Edrina is beginning to cry but trying very hard
not to

**Sally**    You think so?

**Edrina**    Yes

**Sally**    When you got to the UK you lived and worked
somewhere in London
but you don't know where

**Edrina**    Yes

**Sally**    And you were forced to have sex with men for
money?

**Edrina**    Yes

**Sally**    Did you get any of the money?
Look if you're going to cry
we can take a break

**Edrina**    No because I was paying back a debt

**Sally**    What debt?
You've not mentioned a debt before
why are you only mentioning it now?

**Edrina**    I owed Alek's friend
the one I told you about with the van
some money
because he has my brother

**Sally**    What do you mean?

**Edrina**    Alek's friend
he has my brother
Edon

**Sally**    No no
I meant
now you say Alek's friend had a 'van'
when originally you said he had a 'car'.
This isn't adding up I'm afraid

**Edrina**    It was a,
how do you say it
like – a big car

**Sally**    Okay – just let me make a note of that
*A big car.*
And what about your brother?

**Edrina**    They have my brother
Edon
I have to give them money to look after my brother
so he can eat

**Sally**    And Alek
What did he do – about this situation?

**Edrina**    At first he told me he was going to help me and
Edon escape from home

**Sally**    Why did you want to escape your home?

*Beat.*

**Sally**    You need to tell me or I can't help you

**Narrator**    Edrina starts tracing the circular marks on the
table with her finger.
She is beginning to feel a dull ache over her left eye
and with it, her peripheral vision is beginning to go blurry

**Edrina**    My father he –
I can't talk about it

**Sally**    Right we'll have to come back to that then
and when you were 'working' here
were you allowed to leave your accommodation?

**Edrina**    At first no
but after some time yes
they began to trust me so I was let out to the shops and things

**Sally**    Ah so this is the thing, if you were able to go to 'the shops and things'
why didn't you run for help
find the police
tell a member of the public,
anything?

**Edrina**    I thought that if I ran
they would kill Edon
I
I

**Narrator**    Edrina is becoming very distressed

**Sally**    Okay – if you really need us to take a break we can.
I only have a few more questions

**Edrina**    I'm fine keep going

**Sally**    Thank you.
You thought they would kill your brother
do you have any evidence for that?

**Edrina**    They said they would

**Sally**    Who are they?

**Edrina**    Alek's boss – I don't know their names

**Sally**    Why don't you know their names?

**Edrina**    Because they didn't tell me – I

**Sally**    I understand this is difficult for you
but I need the truth.
Did Alek take you from your home, away from your parents
or did you go of your own accord?

**Edrina**    Accord?

**Sally**    It means did you want to go with Alek? Did you choose to go?

**Edrina**   At that time, I went with him because he said that
he loved me and that we were going to get married and my
father said I had to
so I don't know if that's a choice
choosing
is it?

**Sally**   We'll have to see

**Narrator**   She looks through her papers

**Sally**   Nearly there, three more questions.
One) – do you have marks on your skin?

**Edrina**   Excuse me?

**Sally**   Do you have bruises or marks from injuries you have
sustained on your travels?

**Edrina**   Yes

**Sally**   Okay – we'll need a doctor to look at those.
And Two) – did you keep a diary?

**Edrina**   A diary?

**Sally**   To make notes of what has happened to you – it's
quite useful we find

**Edrina**   No – no I didn't

**Sally**   Fine.
And Three) – have you had any counselling?

**Edrina**   No

**Sally**   Okay so that's us done
oh hang on I always forget this one
it's over the page.
Do you have nightmares?

**Narrator**   Edrina looks up and into Sally's eyes for the first
time

**Edina**   Sorry, what?

**Sally**    Do you have nightmares? At night?
Do you dream about these bad things that have happened to
you?

**Edrina**    I haven't slept peacefully for seven years


### Scene Two – Warming

**Narrator**    Edrina leaves the Home Office interview and
walks to a Costa Coffee nearby.
She's in a daze
and can't think about getting on a train.
So she finds an empty table and sits down.
The table is wonky and also has water marks like the table in
the interview.
She looks at the empty chair opposite her and suddenly
something odd happens
Edrina hears her mum's voice
as if her mum is sitting on the chair opposite.
She recalls a conversation they once had, over the kitchen
table
when Edrina was fifteen
where Mum said

**Mum**    Your father says this boy
Alek
likes you

**Edrina**    Does he?

**Mum**    Yes
have you met Alek?

**Edrina**    I don't think so

**Mum**    I didn't think you had
your father – he's strange

**Edrina**    That's one way to put it Mum
I think he's a shit

**Mum**   Don't speak about your father like that! Where did you learn this word?

**Edrina**   Him – he says it a lot

*Beat.*

**Edrina**   Do you like him Mum?

**Mum**   Who?

**Edrina**   My father

**Mum**   What do you mean?

**Edrina**   Well you know
do you like him? As a person.

**Mum**   No
not really.
But I trust him.

**Edrina**   Why? He's a monster to you

**Mum**   Don't be rude Edrina –
he's always provided for us.
Reality can't be perfect
you'll learn that as you get older

**Narrator**   The memory fades away and Edrina continues to trace the marks on the table
and then she recalls
this conversation
with her father
where he said

**Father**   You know what Edrina
it's about time you got out of this house
you're an expense
and you spend too much time with your mother – it's sad.
I've found someone for you, he's a friend of my friend.
He's coming over tomorrow
and his name is Alek

**Edrina** (*to audience*)    Me and Mum made cakes in
preparation.
I made Edon taste test them and he described them, with a
smile, as 'moderately good'.
My father was out when Alek knocked on the door
so Edon answered
and Edon was really good at being the man of the house
it made me feel so proud of my little brother.
We all sat in the living room and Mum brought in the cakes
on a big tray
and then Mum had a cough, she couldn't stop coughing and
she had to leave the room.
So Edon told funny stories about me, to Alek
like about this time when I had accidentally set fire to my
hair with a broken lighter
and how I sang very seriously in the shower – he did an
impression of me
it was embarrassing and also funny.
And towards the end of the conversation Edon started
saying things like he was a grown up

**Edon**    You better take care of my big sister

**Edrina**    It was really sweet.
He was trying to be a man even though he was only thirteen.
I suppose, if you think about it, I was trying to be a woman,
and I was only fifteen.
We all sat on the carpet and played candy crush, taking it in
turns on Alek's phone.
Then Alek had to leave and as he was leaving he said to me

**Alek**    Thank you Edrina
that was the best time I've had in a very long time

**Edrina**    And then the next day
My father said

**Father**    Alek wants to take you out for a date
you better do this right

**Edrina**    And all I could think was
I have no idea how to do a date right so I thought about
things I had seen in movies.
And then the date really was like a movie
which sounds so cheesy
when I say it out loud
but that's what it was like.
He had a beaten-up old sports car and we drove to a bar by
the river
and it was the first time I have ever felt the effect of alcohol
and I could suddenly see why grownups drink it
we found a spot on the banks of the river that no one could
see
there were lots of brambles and washed up at the side of the
river
it was so random
there was this plastic laminated calendar of that year. 2016.
It was big – like A3 – maybe from an office.
As I was looking at all the dates and all the numbers
Alek was lying down staring at the tops of the trees
and he said

**Alek**    Sometimes I get scared that I'm going to spend my
life here
stuck in this shit hole

**Edrina**    Me too

**Alek**    I've got a friend
he says he can get us a job and somewhere to live in Italy

**Edrina**    What?

**Alek**    Yeah

**Edrina**    You've only just met me

**Alek**    I know, but I know

**Edrina**    Know what?

**Alek**    That you're the one for me

**Edrina**   How do you know that?

**Alek**   Because I just do

**Edrina**   And then he kissed me and said

**Alek**   I will always look after you
I will never think bad things about you Edrina, I promise

**Edrina**   And I believed him and I still do

**Narrator**   Edrina has remained in her wooden chair in
Costa Coffee as she is flooded with memories
the noise of the coffee being ground is invading her
her stomach is moving in circles
she stands up and goes outside for some air.
She looks down at her feet
and notices that they look weird – like they don't belong to
her
she hears her mum again

**Mum**   I think it'll all be fine but take this
it's a phone number for a private phone to call me on
wherever you are
find a way to call me but only in the mornings when you
know your dad will be out

**Edrina**   Why can't I call you on the house phone?

**Mum**   Don't ask stupid questions Edrina

**Narrator**   Edrina has got to the end of the street
the circles in her stomach are making her dizzy
she sits down on a bench.
She remembers saying goodbye to Edon
and the last thing he said

**Edon**   I'm going to really miss you
but don't worry I'll look after Mum

**Scene Three – Growing**

**Narrator**    To try and stop the dizziness she focuses on her own feet
she's wearing flip flops and notices that the left flip flop has broken.
And her big toe is bleeding.
The memories invade her again

**Edrina**    When Alek next came to the house
he had bought me a light tan colour suitcase on wheels
with bright white handles
I practised wheeling it around the kitchen
listening to the beautiful sound the wheels made on the floor
they whizzed so smoothly.
It just sounded like freedom.

Two days later
Alek picked me up in his car
and as I hugged Mum goodbye
she said the thing about the phone number again
that she had hidden in my pyjamas.
I thought she's being crazy
because at that moment
leaving that house with Alek
we were in love
totally in love
it was the best thing that had ever happened to me

**Narrator**    Edrina looks up from her feet and stares into the London sky
which is grey
with small bits of blue

**Edrina**    We drove for a long time and then it got dark.
Alek said

**Alek**    Do you mind if we go and pick up my mate on the way?
you'll like him.
He's a good person to know

**Edrina**   Sure, I said.
We met Alek's mate in a forest
with the tallest and oldest-looking trees I had ever seen
I could just about see the tops of them waving in the sky.
It was dark and the only light was a man standing by another car
his face lit up by his phone.
Alek opened the passenger door, to let me out
and a packet of chewing gum fell out onto the ground
I tried to pick it up
but Alek
he kicked it under the car

**Narrator**   She moves her eyes across from her feet
and stares at three old pieces of chewing gum
glued to the pavement

**Edrina**   I still don't know why he didn't let me pick up the chewing gum.
We got into the back of his friend's van
the big car thing
and I asked
where are we going?

**Alek**   We've changed our plans my love
we're going to get the ferry and then get the plane

**Edrina**   Why?

**Alek**   It doesn't matter

**Edrina** (*to audience*)   His voice changed when he said
'it doesn't matter'
it was a different voice

**Narrator**   The dizziness Edrina is experiencing is increasing
as is the sharp piercing pain over her left eye

**Edrina**   We were on the ferry for a long time
and when we drove off it was very cold
I looked out the window at the dark sea

and he put his arm around me in the back of the car
and gave me a little bit of vodka.
We drove for maybe three hours and then we got to this
house
Alek ran around to open the car door for me and gave me
my suitcase.
The sounds of the wheels on the pavement were reassuring
I saw Mum and the kitchen at home
and the white handles of the kitchen cupboards
and then Alek knocked on this green front door
and it was opened by a woman who looked so tired
she had the biggest round dark circles I had ever seen.
Like black holes.
And then she took my suitcase from me
it was all so quick
I couldn't take it
she pushed me into a room off the corridor and locked the
door.
Alek shouted through the door

**Alek**    Edrina, I don't know what's happening
but I promise it'll be okay
I'll sort it out

**Narrator**    She stands up from the bench and starts to walk
it's hard because her flip flop is broken
she takes a few steps and as she does she passes a woman
with round dark circles enveloping her eyes too
and she whispers to her

**Edrina**    Has this happened to you? If I told you, would you
believe me?

**Narrator**    The woman with the dark circles goes into a
charity shop opposite
and Edrina decides to follow her.
The shop's rails are full of beautiful clothes
categorised by colour
the woman starts looking through the black and silver
evening wear.

Edrina passes her and moves to the back of the shop where
she sees two racks of women's shoes and a label that reads
'Five pounds each'.
She feels in her bag for her ASPEN card – given to her by
her caseworker.
The Home Office puts forty pounds and eighty-five pence
on it per week.
Today she has eighteen pounds and thirty-two pence left.
She looks at the shoes
and without realising
does the maths out loud

**Edrina**    Eighteen pounds thirty-two, take away five pounds
is thirteen pounds thirty-two
to last for three more days

**Narrator**    She picks up a pair of new-ish looking black
espadrilles
she chooses these because
she can't afford socks too and hopefully these won't rub
and she goes to the till, pays and leaves.
She chucks her old flip flops in a bin outside.
The cut on her left toe is very painful as she puts the new
shoes on
and then she continues to walk down the road

**Scene Four – Watering**

**Edrina**    In that room off the corridor
there was a bed and one wooden cupboard.
I opened the cupboard and there were seven yellow plastic
hangers
and on the hangers was lingerie
and I realised the lingerie was for me.
I stared at it on the hangers
between the men
and after some time

I could see myself
hanging from the rail too

**Narrator**   She walks for maybe ten minutes until she notices
that she has a dull ache in her womb
her period is starting
and she is also very thirsty.
Edrina goes into Tesco Express to buy a packet of sanitary
towels
and she looks at all the different options and at the pricing
on the yellow labels
subtracting all the prices in her head from thirteen pounds
and thirty-two pence
the pain over her left eye is getting sharper and sharper
she is flooded with noises and voices from Italy
Now the pain is spreading across her forehead.
She leaves Tesco quickly without buying anything and leans
on the shop window

**Edrina**   People have asked me how long I was there
in that room
but the truth is
I don't know
I couldn't follow time.
I had no clock or calendar or watch or phone
to make sense of time.
All these things that you have.
I know every few months maybe
Alek would come to see me and he would say

**Alek**   You won't be here much longer
we'll go together to somewhere else
it'll be better

**Edrina**   How can I trust you
you lied to me – you

**Alek**   Edrina I didn't
they lied to me
they've got me working

but I'll get us out of this
I promise
we'll both get out of this and live in a better place and have a
better life
I promise, they're controlling me too
you just have to trust me.
Keep your faith
please

**Edrina** (*to audience*)    If you had heard him
you'd have believed him too

**Narrator**    She goes back into Tesco
she really needs water and the sanitary towels
and she walks around the shop anti-clockwise
completely unable to block out the memories of the room in
Italy

**Edrina**    Every morning this woman
would come into my room and she would do my face and
body.
She would paint me with brown makeup and would use
powder from a glittery black pot to cover the bruises on my
body.
Sometimes if they were bad she would use face paint from a
tube
just like the one Mum used.
She would stick fake eyelashes on me.
I can still see the glue in the corner of my eyes
she never looked me in the eye
just around my eyes like the glue

And then one day Alek
he came with my suitcase
and said

**Alek**    Come on we're leaving

**Edrina**    He explained this time that finally we were going
to get on a plane and come to the UK and start our happy
life.

He opened the green front door and we just walked out of
the house and into his car.
He gave me a passport that wasn't mine
a woman called Kirsty Reed.
I had to practise saying her name out loud and her date of
birth
Kirsty Reed. 24th September 2001.

**Alek**    I'm so proud of you Kirsty
I knew we'd get out of this together

**Edrina**    I'd never been to an airport
Alek bought me sunglasses in a shop that also sold
newspapers.
I saw the date on the top right
And I just couldn't believe it
2019. It was now 2019.
I'd been in that room for three years

*Beat.*

I put my sunglasses on my head like real people do in airports
I wheeled my suitcase on the beautiful white floor and I
thought of how finally when we get to the UK
I'll phone Mum.
Then at the airport they must have seen something on the
screen
they took me into a small room
I had to open up my bag and this woman with glasses
unfolded everything that Mum had folded
I could smell Mum's perfume on the clothes
and when she got to my pyjamas
the piece of paper with Mum's number on it – fell out
she picked it up and then she put it back
and then she looked at me and said –

**Airport Security Woman**    What's your name?

**Edrina**    Kirsty Reed

**Airport Security Woman**    All okay, I just needed to check
enjoy your holiday

**Edrina**    And she looked at me
right in the eye
and I couldn't look at her.
So I lowered my eyes and stared at the white floor

We took an easyJet flight to London Gatwick.
As we sat waiting to get on the plane Alek put his arm
around me
and I saw our reflection in the window
and we looked like – just like such normal people

**Narrator**    In the present, right now, she's still in Tesco
and still very thirsty and starts to look for the water
she moves quickly until she has standing in front of a fridge
full of soft drinks

**Edrina**    Flying on a plane – to be so high in the blue skies
The closest to God I'd ever been.
Alek held my hand for take off and landing
he was so kind.
We had no problem with security
they'd made the passport – with my picture – I don't know
how but they had
but it meant we could travel so simply.
It was like it was all
the easiest thing in the world.


**Scene Five – Lighting**

**Narrator**    She chooses a bottle of water
the cheapest available which is seventy-nine pence.
And a packet of sanitary towels
one pound fifty – also the cheapest available
and she goes to the checkout to pay.
She stands in the queue

**Edrina**   We went to a carpark on a bus and met another
one of Alek's friends
We got into a car and in the back of the car
when Alek
he suddenly turned to me and he was panicky and he said

**Alek**   I'm sorry
they're making me do it
I don't know what to do

**Narrator**   Edrina is now at the front of the queue in Tesco
the pain has spread across her head and now down the back
of her neck
her heart is racing and she is shaking, cold.
Out of the corner of her right eye she thinks she can see Alek.
She turns quickly to try and see him

If you were standing behind her in the queue
you'd think
this person isn't well
every bit of her says this.
She goes forward and gives the water and the sanitary towels
to the person behind the counter.
She pays.
Eleven pounds and three pence left.
She leaves and continues to walk

**Edrina**   We drove through the streets of London
Alek sat next to me and I realised tears were falling silently
from his eyes
I squeezed his hand and prayed to God
I knew God would hear me, God would hear us.
We arrived on a street with lots of houses and at the end of
the street was like an industrial estate
it had a big wire gate that opened for us
it reminded me of the water pump building at home.
And I was pulled out of the car by Alek's friend
I can't really remember what happened next and how it all
happened
until I was in the room

This room was underground with one very bright strip light
on the ceiling.
There was a mattress on the floor and the door had a silver
handle
with a small lock that clicked.
Sort of like something you'd expect to find in an office.
The things that happened in that room are not what you can
say.
There are no words to describe what happened to my body
to my mind
and to my soul.

Maybe after one week or two
I didn't know the time
I got to the point
that that – yeah –
I'm ashamed of
that I didn't want to live
I wanted to be dead.
I didn't want to be here.

So I started screaming and I kept screaming.
They gagged me but I kept screaming.
I vomited but I kept screaming.
Eventually Alek he came and said

**Alek**    Edrina please you have to be quiet you have to stop
– stop it

**Edrina**    And then he hit me,
he hadn't ever done this before
he was very stressed and he was crying again.
Then he got out his phone and he went to this website
and he showed me this long page of many squares
many many squares
and in each square was a human.
He scrolled through so many and then he clicked on one of
the pictures and there was
Edon
my little brother

he was wearing a white t-shirt and a pair of shorts.
And underneath it just said one word
'Young.'

He was for sale too

And then Alek explained

**Alek**   I'm sorry Edrina but they have Edon
I'm going to help him but
you have to help me

**Narrator**   Edrina sees another bench and has to sit down
the noises
voices
memories in her head are completely overwhelming.
She can't move so she sits and stares at the crack where the
pavement meets the road
and she sees
a tiny green weed that is growing there.
On its own.
One stem of green with two little leaves
it's miniscule
but it is there


**Scene Six – Finding**

**Narrator**   Time moves and Edrina is still sitting on the
bench
she has drunk half a bottle of the seventy-nine-pence water
that's almost exactly one per cent of her weekly income.
Occasionally she has looked up at the people walking by
none of them have looked at her because they're all
engrossed in their phones

**Edrina**   Maybe they're looking at Edon
maybe they know how to find him

**Narrator**   If someone wants to meet Edon they can find
him very easily
but they'll have to pay first

**Edrina**    Alek knows where Edon is

**Narrator**    Edrina can't think about anything else other than

**Edrina**    Where is Edon?

**Narrator**    Over and over again
where is Edon? Where is Edon?
She presses her hands against her forehead

**Edrina**    Once I knew they had him
I behaved better
I was quiet and did what they said
and after a few months I was given a different room with a
window
where you could see a bit of sky
and the top of a very large tree
I'd watch it for hours
the branches waving at me.
And I made friends with one of the security guards
he was kinder than the others.
Then one afternoon
we went in a car with blacked-out windows to a big
supermarket
that was near a reservoir
and I imagined diving head first into the freezing water.
He gave me money and I bought some deodorant
toothpaste and a five-pack of cotton underwear
the lacey ones they made me wear gave me eczema
and my skin was raw
so I got cream for that too

**Narrator**    And then suddenly
cutting through this memory
she hears Sally in the Home Office interview

**Sally**    Why didn't you run for help? Find the police, tell a
member of the public, anything?

**Edrina**    And the truth is
of course I thought about running.

I'm not an idiot
but I didn't know what they would do to Edon if I ran.
So I stayed with the security guard in the shop.
I followed him like a little girl.
And maybe this makes me stupid
but at the time I had no choice.
I didn't know about choices
I have never ever had them.
Choice is not what people like me have

**Narrator**   Edrina is beginning to feel huge waves of anger
she can feel it like sand in her blood
and the pounding in her head will not stop
she hears Sally again

**Sally**   We shall have to see

**Edrina**   Every day and every night
the security guard
stood just inside the main front door.
There were many rooms
they kept the girls separate mainly
but the security guard
he wore a suit and he had a ear piece – that was fake – I
never saw him use it
but I think it helped the clients feel
safer
and he sometimes would let three of us use the kitchen to
maybe
make a drink or something
and the girls I saw there
so many different ones
we were all different shapes and colours and textures
and it made me think of the different squares on the website
where Edon was
where Edon is.

I started making this security guard coffee for his shift
he said I made good coffee
and he'd let me smoke with him at the back door

and then one day when we were smoking
I asked him if he knew where my suitcase was
and I said it's because it had a jumper in there that would
help me sleep.
He was still for a moment
I thought he was going to laugh in my face and then he said

**Security Guard**   Fine – I can show you

**Edrina**   We walked down the stairs and he opened another
door with a silver handle
it wasn't even locked
this room
it was
there were hundreds
maybe thousands of bags that had just been thrown in on
top of one another

**Security Guard**   Go and find it

**Edrina**   I walked in
I had to climb on top of bags and to move others to make a
path for myself.
Some of them were very heavy
all of them had the airline tags still on them.
I imagined all those people with sunglasses on their head
thinking they were starting a new life. I got all the way to the
back wall of the room that was dripping with damp
when the security guard shouted

**Security Guard**   Hurry up!
Two minutes or I'm going to get in trouble and so will you

**Edrina**   I started clawing at the bags underneath me
pulling at any handle I could find
and then I saw it out of the corner of my eye
I saw the bright white handle.
I grabbed it and pulled it out.
Opened it up, the smell was my home
I grabbed my pink hoodie and unfolded my pyjamas
and got the piece of paper that was tucked in the right hand
pocket.

Closed up the bag and scrambled out.
The security guard was really angry by this point

**Security Guard**    Get back in your room!

**Edrina**    I ran up the stairs and into my room, he locked the door and
I was punished for a long time after that
I don't know why,
I guess he felt angry with himself for letting me do it.
No food for three days
when I got half a tuna sandwich
but it didn't matter
I had the number so nothing else really mattered.
The number on the paper kept me alive

**Scene Seven – Loving**

**Narrator**    Back in London
today
she's still sitting on the bench
pressing her forehead into her hands.
All she can hear is the past.
The present is gone.

**Edrina**    It took a long time until I was in the kitchen with Samira

**Narrator**    People are continuing to walk past her on the street

**Edrina** (*looking at the narrator for the first time*)    Samira was one of the main girls
she'd been there a long time
and they trusted her
she had an iPhone and two laptops and
she organised the bookings on a big spreadsheet.
We were all squares on her screen too.
If you were in the kitchen together she'd play music from the radio on her phone
Samira was sometimes nice and sometimes not nice

you'd never know what mood she'd be in
so I decided to come straight out with it
and said
'Hey Samira'
and she said

**Samira**   Hey

**Edrina**   Can I borrow your phone please?

**Samira**   What the – what did you say?

**Edrina**   Can I borrow your phone please?
I want to call my mum

**Samira**   Are you joking?

**Edrina**   No, I'm serious. I just want to tell her that – that
I'm fine.
I won't say anything about where I am
I just want to hear her voice

*Beat.*

Please

**Samira**   I will give you one minute and if you do anything
I will double your clients and you won't leave your room for
a month.
Understand?

**Edrina**   So I get the piece of paper out and press the
numbers.
It rang three times
and I couldn't believe it
because it'd been so long
she picked up

**Mum**   Hello?

**Edrina**   Hi Mum it's me

**Mum**   Edrina?

**Edrina**   Yeah it's me

**Mum**    I can't – I can't believe it.
Six years and you only just call me

*Beat.*

**Edrina**    I haven't known how long
this is this first time I've had a phone
my friend is letting me borrow this one

**Mum**    What about Edon?

**Edrina**    I don't know where he is

**Mum**    What do you mean?
Where's Alek?

**Edrina**    I don't know
we broke up I think

**Mum**    Are you alright
you sound different

**Edrina**    I'm – I'm fine Mum
it's just been a long time

**Narrator**    She feels herself starting to cry and then Samira
says

**Samira**    Time's up

**Narrator**    So Edrina says

**Edrina**    I'm all good
it's just nice to hear your voice

**Mum**    Are you sure you're alright?

**Narrator**    Edrina can hear Mum panicking and shouting
and then. Samira grabs the phone and hangs up

**Edrina**    And all I could see was –

**Edrina** *and the* **Narrator** *look at each other for the first time.*

**Narrator**    Do you want to do this bit?

**Edrina**    Yes

**Narrator**    Okay I'm still here

**Edrina**    And all I could see was Mum lying on the kitchen
floor screaming

And that was it


## Scene Eight – Choosing

**Narrator**    Tears are now falling from her eyes

**Edrina**    I don't know what or why exactly
but when I heard Mum just
I can't describe it.
I knew I had two options
either I was going to die in that room
or I was going to get out and I decided that Mum would
have wanted me to run

I waited a few weeks until I was in the kitchen alone.
I made the security guard a coffee and I walked down the
stairs to give it to him
he gave me a cigarette
I waited till he had lit his and then
then I ran.
I could hear him shouting and then I could hear Samira
screaming at him
I just kept running I didn't have shoes and each object that
hurt me
I thanked
because it meant I was still alive

I ran into the first shop I saw on a busy road
rolls of fabric were leaning against the walls.
And this woman she was in there – behind the counter –
she looked so tired
again with dark circles and I said

Please, please, help me

And then she bolted the door.
And for a few moments I thought she was one of them
but she called the police and
I sat on the floor and waited

*Part Two*

*Mind*

## Scene One – Thinking

**Narrator**   One hundred and fifty-two days ago
That's nearly five months ago
Edrina she realised
or she choose
or she knew
she had to run

**Edrina**   The police took me to an interview room
and gave me a pair of flip flops
and they asked me so many questions
I couldn't answer because I kept vomiting

They called the Salvation Army to come and pick me up.
I thought it was the army army and that they were going to
put me in prison.
But actually it was a volunteer who took me to a Safe House
they asked me a lot of questions
I think they were trying to be nice
but it was impossible for me to

**Volunteer** (*cutting in*)   Who brought you here?
Do you know their names?
Have you got this leaflet?
Can you call these numbers?
Do you have a phone?

**Edrina**   And I just couldn't answer because my head
I thought it was going to explode with pain.
All I could say was

Where is Edon?

I went in the car with the volunteer
and I vomited again

I cleared it up the best I could and said sorry
I was so embarrassed

**Narrator**    Five days after Edrina ran
she gave permission for her case to be referred to the
National Referral Mechanism
also known as
the NRM

**Edrina**    The NRM
it's this mechanism
like a machine I guess
that identifies and referers potential victims of modern
slavery in the UK
I'm in the machine now

**Narrator**    It's taken one hundred and fifty-two days to get
to the Home Office interview that took place today
and during that time she has received
a Reasonable Grounds Letter that was sent to her Safe
House

**Edrina**    It says that some people agree there are
Reasonable Grounds to believe me
when I say
I've been a victim of trafficking.
Now I'm waiting for a Conclusive Grounds letter – which
says they believe me.
But I don't think the Home Office believes me
so

**Narrator**    She's met a caseworker every two weeks at her
Safe House
and she's seen a GP once
who in a ten-minute consultation
was able to diagnose that she'd suffered severe sexual assult
over a long period of time.
But these notes had not got to the Home Office
an administrative error

**Edrina**    I am on a waiting list for therapy that's five
hundred and forty-seven days long

**Narrator**    Because of the abuse she's suffered since she was child
she doesn't know how to operate as a person
she's never been treated like one, so how would she?
She doesn't know how to make decisions
because she's never been allowed to

**Edrina**    So now I don't
I don't know what to do

**Narrator**    Three hours pass
she is still sitting on the bench
reliving the Home Office interview over and over again

*Beat.*

*The* **Narrator** *speaks directly to* **Edrina**.

**Narrator**    Edrina, can you still hear me?

**Edrina**    Yes

**Narrator**    How are you feeling?

**Edrina**    I don't know
I don't know anymore
I think I should
I just don't think there is any point to it anymore

**Narrator**    Any point to what?

**Edrina**    Me and my life
nobody cares

**Narrator**    Your mum cares about you, she loves you

**Edrina**    But I can never see her again because
I can't go back
I can't

**Narrator**    It's okay Edrina

**Edrina**    It's not
no part of this is okay

**Narrator**    You just have to hold on
and something good will happen
I promise

She sits on the bench for another hour
and then a woman with a friendly face and blonde hair
approaches her
and she says

**Woman**    Are you alright?
You were here when I walked passed earlier and I thought
I'd better check

**Narrator**    Edrina says nothing

**Woman**    Have you eaten recently? You look a bit–
are you feeling unwell?

**Edrina**    I'm fine

**Woman**    There's a cafe round the corner
I'd like to buy you something
I'll bring it back here
hang on

**Narrator**    Edrina says nothing.
The woman leaves and comes back with a cheese toastie and
a cup of tea

**Woman**    Here you go

**Narrator**    Edrina takes it

**Edrina**    Thank you

**Narrator**    She unfolds the warm paper wrapper
she's still feeling nauseous and her head is splitting with pain
but she hasn't eaten since yesterday so this is probably a
good idea.
She takes one bite and the woman says

**Woman**    You poor thing – do you live round here?

**Edrina**    No

**Woman**    What brings you here then?

**Edrina**    I just had a meeting with the Home Office

**Woman**    Oh, one of their buildings is round the corner isn't it?

**Edrina**    Yeah

**Woman**    Do you have a job?

**Edrina** (*laughing*)    No

**Woman**    Why is that funny?

**Edrina**    I'm not allowed a job

**Woman**    What do you mean? Everyone's got to work

**Edrina**    Not me
I can't work because I'm in this machine
to try and prove that I've been in slavery

**Woman**    That sounds – try and prove what sorry?

**Edrina**    Prove that
I've been a slave
and whilst I'm in this system the people in control say I can't work

**Woman**    Why?

**Edrina**    I don't know maybe because I'm stealing jobs from people who are
more important than me
that are better than me

**Woman**    That doesn't sound right
I'm sure that's not the case

**Edrina**    Well that's what's happening

**Woman**    Do you have money?

**Edrina**    I have eleven pounds and three pence to last the next three days

**Woman**    That's not enough

*Beat.*

**Woman**    Would you like to come to my house?
I live two tube stops away
I'll pay

**Narrator**    Edrina goes with the woman with the friendly
face and blonde hair.
Maybe this is the good thing that was supposed to happen


### Scene Two – Surviving

**Narrator**    What happens next is complex and simple,
simultaneously.
It also happens to around half of the people in the National
Referral Mechanism.
Not exactly like this each time, this is one of the less dramatic
and violent versions.
The woman with the friendly face and blonde hair
takes Edrina back to her house and offers Edrina a bed for
the night

**Woman**    Here you go
I've two other friends staying too
and they work for me

**Edrina**    Doing what?

**Woman**    Cleaning – I've a business
let's talk about it later
the most important thing is that you rest

**Edrina**    Okay, thank you

**Narrator**    The woman leaves Edrina in the room.
It has a small single bed with clean white sheets.
Edrina lies down and closes her eyes and tries to think

**Edrina**    I feel like I could sleep forever

**Narrator**   She sleeps for three hours straight and is woken up by the woman
with the friendly face and blonde hair
bringing her a cup of tea

**Woman**   I'm glad you slept
you don't need to make a decision right now
but if you want to stay and work for me you'd be very welcome.
You'd start off as a trainee and then we'd see how it's going
cash in hand

**Edrina**   What do you pay?

**Woman**   We'll negotiate that further down the line

**Narrator**   Edrina doesn't know what to do
but she does know that this bed feels nice
and this woman isn't totally bad

**Edrina**   I don't know

**Woman**   Well don't worry about that for the moment
let's just see

**Narrator**   Within three weeks Edrina is re-trafficked.
She's working for five pounds a day and she has no control over her own life,
no documentation,
no phone,
no nothing.

**Edrina**   It's not as bad as it was before.
But the woman
she changed over time
she controls everything
and now
I

**Narrator**   It was very easy for the woman to target Edrina
she is intensely vulnerable and that sort of vulnerability
can be spotted and smelled by those who wish to exploit or
who have no choice but to exploit.

So

Edrina, can you still hear me?

*Beat.*

Edrina?

**Edrina** *looks at the* **Narrator** *and nods.*

**Narrator**   Okay let's go back to the beginning.
To the Home Office interview where Sally was sitting on one
side of the table
and Edrina on the other

**Sally**   Well here's the problem Edrina,
the law in this country doesn't work with stories
it only works with facts.
And to put it simply, your story – look it just isn't credible

**Narrator**   How did that make you feel Edrina?

**Edrina**   I couldn't really feel anything at that point
I felt numb
and like I wasn't there

**Narrator**   What do you mean you weren't there?
You were there

**Edrina**   I can't describe it.
I just went somewhere else

**Narrator**   Where?

**Edrina**   I can't describe it

**Narrator**   Try

**Edrina**   I can't

**Narrator**   Can anyone else?

**Kerry Smith**, *CEO of the Helen Bamber Foundation, stands up
from her seat in the audience and speaks.*

**Kerry**   I can.

**Narrator**   This is Kerry. She's not an actor, she's CEO of the Helen Bamber Foundation.

**Kerry**   When Edrina walked into that small room with a person behind a desk
she was feeling scared, an emotion she lives with constantly. Feeling scared means that
the part of her brain important for self-protection
the amygdala
went into overdrive
causing her heart to race and her breathing to become shallow.
The small dark room reminded her of rooms she had been imprisoned in.
The silver door handle to the Home Office and the click as it shut
turned into that same silver door handle from the room on the industrial estate somewhere in London. Edrina's brain has become used to responding to abuse and this has meant that a feeling of fear
or physical arousal or a sound
can unleash a cascade of memories of the trauma she has experienced.
These memories are different from normal memories in that they are re-experienced as if they are happening again right now, with all of the danger and fear coming again right at this moment. It doesn't feel like the past, which is when it really happened,
because they are so vivid
they can overwhelm and stun you.
Edrina dissociated
her brain disconnected from her current experience
and she stopped being aware of where she was in time and space.
She was back there in the helplessness of the past
re-living it as if it was happening again now

**Edrina**   I heard Sally say

**Sally**    And to put it simply, your story – look it just isn't credible

**Kerry**    And what happened then?

**Edrina**    I felt like there was barbed wire in my ears and my throat
and it made me realise that I don't think anyone has ever believed me.
The way she said it made me think of my father
the dismissiveness was the same.
They don't trust me and I don't trust them

**Kerry**    That sounds very painful

**Edrina**    When people ask me questions about what's happened
it's very difficult to make my thoughts in order

**Kerry**    Can you explain that a little more?

**Edrina**    When I think about the things that have happened
they get very blurry
like I can't hold on to them
they slip away from me
and join together in a muddle
in the wrong order
so when Sally said

**Sally**    You think so?

**Edrina**    I couldn't remember where I'd been and what order things have happened in
in my head I see them
but saying them out loud is different

**Kerry**    When you ask a person directly about traumatic events
they may not recall them as anything other than snapshots of sensations
or images
it is common for the memory to be hazy and confused.

This can be another way they've learnt to survive
or because the memory is so traumatic it has been shut away
by the brain
rather than properly organised like a normal bad memory
would be.
It is vital to demonstrate sensitivity when approaching
distressing questions
and to start where the person is
for example Sally could have said

**Sally**   I have some questions about the places you have been.
Would it be okay if we talked about those places that you can
remember?

**Kerry**   It feels very different

**Edrina**   I don't think anyone understands the power those
people have over me. And Edon

**Kerry**   So when Sally said

**Sally**   Did you get any of the money?

**Kerry**   And

**Sally**   Where is Edon?

**Kerry**   What happened then Edrina?

**Edrina**   All I felt was that the barbed wire in my ears and
throat
had set on fire
and now it was in my chest and stomach
and that I should've stayed to save Edon.
All I could see was Edon in the square box on that website

**Kerry**   Edrina has been conditioned by the traffickers to
believe she is responsible for her brother's wellbeing
something that has most likely existed in her since she was
born.
So they are manipulating that love to their advantage.
If you tell Edrina she is 'wrong' or that she shouldn't think
that

you are removing all of her agency again.
She needs *time* and the authorities around her need to *take time* to consider her account.
If they discredit her opinions then they are not going to help her recovery
they will only reinforce her feelings of worthlessness.
Sally could instead have said

**Sally**    I understand that you are very worried about your brother, that sounds very hard

**Kerry**    When extremely sensitive information arises in the course of an interview
Survivors' feelings about it need to be acknowledged respectfully.
It seemed that in the interview Edrina was unable to talk about her father

**Edrina**    Please

**Kerry**    One of the many reasons Edrina was vulnerable to Alek
was that she grew up in a highly abusive and dysfunctional home.
It seems that her father was involved in the trafficking of her and her brother.
You can't make sense of this level of betrayal and horror in a fifteen-minute interview

*Beat.*

**Kerry**    Would you like to stop Edrina?

**Edrina**    Yes please

**Kerry**    Let's take a few moments
Edrina let us know if you feel okay to continue

*Beat – everyone stops until* **Edrina** *decides to speak.*

**Edrina**    Okay
it's okay

let's keep going
when Sally said

**Sally**    I understand this is difficult for you
but I need the truth.
Did Alek take you from your home, from your parents
or did you go of your own accord?

**Edrina**    And I said 'Accord?' and she explained

**Sally**    It means did you want to go with Alek? Did you
choose to go?

**Edrina**    I chose to go
because I love him
and I know he loves me

**Kerry**    When vulnerable people are groomed
they don't know they are being groomed.
They believe they are being loved.
That's how grooming works.
But if you say to someone
that the person they love is a predator
without the victim having had time to understand this
themselves
you're actually telling that person that everything they have
ever known is a lie
that the foundations their life has been built on are wrong
and evil and that they are

**Edrina**    Stupid.
And I am bad inside
I am a bad person

**Kerry**    They will feel catastrophic shame
which will present as anger, severe depression and anxiety.
Sally could have said

**Sally**    I understand you feel loyalty to this man, it sounds
very complicated

**Kerry**    And finally when Sally asked

**Sally**    Oh just one more question, I always forget this one, it's last on the list.
Do you have nightmares?

**Kerry**    This question is frequently asked to assess whether potential victims of modern slavery are traumatised by their experiences

**Edrina**    It just felt stupid

**Kerry**    What do you mean?

**Edrina**    Because the nightmares – I wake up from reality is much worse

**Kerry**    We know that the only way to help people recover is to give them time
and to communicate in a calm, kind and consistent way.
It's not Sally's fault, she hasn't been trained
she's not seeing a Survivor
she's seeing a number in a square in a spreadsheet

**Narrator**    What happened to you after that interview, Edrina?

**Edrina**    I lost myself again
I drowned in my memories

**Kerry**    This is how Complex Post Traumatic Stress Disorder works


**Scene Three – Learning**

**Narrator**    One hundred and fifty-two days ago
Edrina became a number in the National Referral Mechanism
and another square on the internet.

**Kerry**    Imagine if she knew how to manage her symptoms of Complex PTSD.
Imagine if she could know her worth.
Imagine if she could express her wants and needs freely.

**Narrator**   Are you saying that these past one hundred and fifty-two days could have gone differently?

**Edrina**   How? How could that have happened?

**Kerry**   Anoushka, can you play another role for us please?

**Anoushka**   Yes, absolutely

**Kerry**   Anoushka is now going to play the role of someone who has been trained with the Trauma Informed Code of Conduct. Someone who is going to be with Edrina from when she is picked up from the fabric shop till now and for the rest of her recovery.
Edrina what would you like to call her?

**Edrina**   I don't know

**Narrator**   Take your time
you can call her anything
something that makes sense to you

*Beat.*

**Edrina**   I don't believe in it
but maybe we should call her
Hope

**Kerry**   Hope. Let's go with that.
Hope arrives at the fabric shop, where Edrina first ran to, with the police and introduces herself before the police do
she shows the police how to take things slowly
to create the illusion of time
to help Edrina calm her nervous system

**Narrator**   Hope establishes whether Edrina needs an interpreter
she also has a bag with her and inside it are
a pair of practical shoes
a warm coat
toiletries

**Edrina**    And instead of taking me to a police station they
take me to this place
which has lots of windows
and sofas
and green, growing plants.
When I get there Hope walks into a room before me and she
lets me follow her

**Hope**    Where would you like to sit?

**Edrina**    I don't know what chair to choose
so I stand there for a long time I think
I choose a small, soft yellow chair
and I notice Hope has left the door open.
No one has ever left the door open before

**Hope**    People will walk past
they are clinicians who work in this charity
you are safe here.
Would you like some water or a hot drink?

**Edrina**    I say 'water please' and she gets me some.
And then we just sit for a bit.
She doesn't stare at me
or ask me lots of questions
she just talks about the things in the room.
There's a painting of clouds in a blue sky
there's a water machine where she got the cool water from
and there's a very slight breeze coming through the open
window and then Hope says

**Hope**    That's a nice breeze

**Edrina**    And for the first time in seven years
I have the smallest moment where
I believe I'm here.
I'm here right now.
I'm in London.
Sitting on a yellow chair.

*Part Three*

*Soul*

### Scene One – Living

**Kerry**   The truth is
it'll take the rest of Edrina's life for her to recover from her experiences.
We know that recovery could happen if she has access to therapeutic, legal, housing and medical aid.
Tools to help her rebuild herself so she can live freely

**Narrator**   So there is a version of events where Edrina is not re-trafficked?

*Beat.*

**Kerry**   Yes
if she'd had more support
then yes

**Narrator**   Let's go back
to when the woman with the friendly face and blonde hair offered her a role as a trainee cleaner for no money

**Edrina**   I've got nothing
it's better than what was happening before I should take this job

**Kerry**   If Edrina had been working with Hope for the past one hundred and fifty-two days discovering things like

**Hope**   I care about your safety

**Edrina**   You care about my safety

**Hope**   You don't have to do anything
you don't want to do

**Edrina**   I don't have to do anything
I don't want to do

**Hope**    If you're experiencing pressure from someone or
you're unsure of something
you can talk to me about it

**Edrina**    If I'm experiencing pressure from someone or if
I'm unsure of something
I can talk to you about it

**Hope**    You are a human
and you have rights
to express yourself and to live freely

**Edrina**    I am a human
I have rights
to express myself and to live freely

**Hope**    Yes

**Kerry**    And from there
everything else follows.
So, Edrina may say to the woman who is trying to exploit her

*Beat.*

**Edrina**    I don't feel comfortable accepting this job from you
right now.
Can I take your phone number and have some time to think
about it?

**Narrator**    And then Edrina stands up and she walks out of
the woman's house
and reaches into her bag
for the phone that Hope has given her
and she calls Hope and
Hope picks up and says

**Hope**    Hi Edrina

**Edrina**    Hi – I was just in this weird situation with this
woman
who was trying to give me a job
but it didn't feel right

**Hope**    Thank you for sharing that with me
what did you do when she said that?

**Edrina**    I told her I felt uncomfortable and that I needed
some time to think about it

**Hope**    How do you feel now?

**Edrina**    A bit weird to be honest

**Hope**    That's understandable

**Edrina**    I didn't want to do that job
and it felt like it wasn't right
yeah I think that's what happened

**Hope**    Yeah – I think so too

**Narrator**    They both organise their next meeting and hang
up.
Edrina puts the phone back in her bag and walks slowly
down the street
looking at her feet as they move.
And then

**Edrina**    And then once I'm sure they are my feet
in my body
a body that belongs to me
and nobody else,
I look up at the sky,
and I
breathe.

Printed in the USA
CPSIA information can be obtained
at www.ICGtesting.com
LVHW012227061023
760368LV00002B/534